Reflections of grief: A parent carer story

By Lisa Reakes

Reflections of Grief: a parent carer story
by Lisa Reakes

First published in 2022 by Close Publications.

Printed by St Andrew's Press of Wells.

Whilst every effort has been made to trace the owners of the copyright material reproduced herein, the publishers would like to apologise for any omissions and will be pleased to incorporate any missing acknowledgements in future editions.

A CIP catalogue record of this book is available from the British Library.

ISBN: 978-1-7399408-4-3

Foreword by Becky Skuse

Why do bad things happen to good people? It's an age-old question that we can't help but ask ourselves at times of tragedy or loss.

We all experience losses, small and big. Some of us will experience sudden tragic loss, the likes of which we could never have imagined. The sort of trauma that shakes our existence to the core.

When this sort of life earthquake happens, time seems to stop. Everything changes inside you, but the world seems the same. We search for answers and guidance, trying to make sense out of what seems so surreal.

Sometimes that search feels like a dark place with no escape. But there is always hope, even if it's only very small and slow to emerge. If your heart is willing and your mind is open, these dark times can lead you to enlightenment.

If we're lucky, we can find other people who have trodden a similar path, through a land of loss and grief. Just like the yellow brick road, their wisdom can help you find a way through this scary new world, to a land of peace and acceptance.

Your life journey is unique to you and only you can walk its path. But you're not alone. My trauma happened in 2016 when my dad died rather suddenly. And three days before my wedding.

Lisa Reakes has been my friend since the early 2000s but since 2016 she's also been an inspiration to me. A good role model doesn't tell you what you should think, feel or do. They help you to realise your own truths and encourage you on your own journey.

Lisa's bravery, resilience, kindness, adaptability and wisdom have been invaluable on my grief journey. Her example has given me hope, strength and belief in the goodness of the human spirit.

In the pages that follow, she outlines her own grief journey with honesty, humility and grace. By sharing her story, I think she offers an abundance of wise insights that will help anyone struggling with trauma.

So why do bad things happen to good people? Lisa has found her answer and her path through grief. The path she was always destined for.

Becky Skuse is a writer, editor, craft tutor and former hypnotherapist. She's written about questions of well-being for various publications, including as editor of Planet Mindful magazine.

Introduction

This book is not intended as a self-help or how to. It is intended as an honest account of how I came to cope and manage in a situation I found intensely difficult and challenging; the acute illness of my daughter aged almost-two, and the resulting life-long disability. I have tried to be as candid as I can, not intending to sugar-coat anything, to tell my story as it appeared to me. That is not to say that I have failed to discover a different perspective, a different way of looking at the same thing, but that took years of hard graft. I have found some peace, I have found some acceptance, I have found some joy, and those were forged through enormous grief.

I have interspersed that story with accounts of my personal history, hoping to demonstrate that those parts of my story helped me to reach my peace and acceptance in this story, as it unfolded. I can see now that I have been learning and growing, building skills that I would need, that I could use to build strength and resilience. However, I cannot hide nor would wish to, that when my daughter became ill, I was entirely compromised as a person emotionally, physically and spiritually. I felt completely shrouded in darkness, it was all I could see. But the light found me and brought me back. That is my story, a story interwoven with grief.

Beginning

When I came into this world, I didn't know what to expect. I did not expect anything. I did not comprehend until much later that I had been born with an intention, I had chosen this life. So, in a way I did know what to expect, but was not consciously aware of it.

My mum told me once that she forgot to feed me one day, when I was a baby. I can't be sure of the truth of this but it makes sense, knowing the dynamic that existed between my mum and my brother. My brother was a baby that didn't want cuddles and cried a lot, by all accounts. So, when I came along 18 months later, I am sure I was intrigued by the zoo in which I had been placed. I can very much imagine how my attention could have been taken up by the ebb and flow of power being played out between my mum and brother. How I might not even have thought of food. I can see that happening very much.

My first clear memory is of my brother's first day at school. I loved my brother and I do remember not wanting him to start school. I wanted him to stay with me. Perhaps I didn't want to be left on my own with my mum? Perhaps.

We had dropped my brother at school and I was going to playschool. I ran the length of the hall to try to get away, to escape. Just at the end of the hall, which seemed enormous, as it would to little me, a woman came out of a door with arms outstretched, I turned tail and made for the main entrance, and I distinctly remember almost making it to freedom when I was caught. I had almost made it. I was so upset. I just wanted to be with my brother.

I can't say that after that, I remember my brother really wanting to be around me or play with me much. But memory isn't always accurate and can be coloured by many flavours. We can bring so much to a memory that may not be entirely true.

We moved to the country just before I started Primary School. I loved it. I loved being close to nature and I now feel a sacred connection to it. Perhaps I did then but I didn't know it?

It didn't suit my mum though, she loved being able to walk to somewhere, to be part of life and more in the thick of it. She wanted people around her to mask her loneliness maybe? Interesting how we can still feel lonely in a crowd. But I've never really felt lonely. I may be alone but I don't feel lonely. What a blessing. The truth is, we are all alone. We each have our own unique experience, and that can make us feel lonely. We can never really connect to another. No-one can ever really understand us. To accept that truth is a relief. Then I don't have to seek that 'one' person who truly understands me intimately. I am really seeking myself. As I am the only one who could ever possibly understand why I have done things, what motivates me and how I think and feel. It's a relief to know I already know the one who understands me best. Or do I know me? I am an infinite being of light and love. I am infinite possibility. So I am really on a voyage of self-discovery this lifetime, as in every lifetime.

I was told the other day that a planetary aspect in my birth natal chart indicates that I have spent many lifetimes wandering and gathering information. I have a wandering and free spirit. This really made sense to me, and that in this lifetime I was drawing together all the strands of experience and distilling them. I was so pleased to hear it. It made me smile to think that I'd been wandering around exploring and experiencing this world, learning and growing. This lifetime I have felt at times confined and restricted by circumstances. I chose that, so that the only avenue for expansion was of my mind. It made sense that I'd earned my self-imposed constriction through lifetimes of freedom and wandering. I still feel that freedom and wandering within me. My mind has no limitation.

It irked me, several years ago, when an acquaintance told me I should go on a vision quest. Inside me arose a distinct 'No! I don't need to do anything of the sort'. We can feel compelled to go looking, searching and seeking. To find what we are looking for. However, I am not convinced that I have to find anything. I don't necessarily have to go seeking it, it can come to me, if I let it. That's not to say that seeking is not a path well-trodden, but I feel strongly it's not my path this lifetime. And now I know why, I've already done it! So, perhaps that is why I had such an aversion to that suggestion. I really did feel at that moment that I could get everything I needed simply by staying right where I was. I didn't need to go anywhere; it was all there within my grasp. I already was going places, in my mind.

Suffering is a most powerful teacher. Better than any drug or vision quest. If you just have the courage to feel the pain, it really can blow your mind. Suffering has shaped me into the person I am today and I am very grateful. Saturn is the planet that rules bereavements and misfortunes. What a powerful teacher. I remain in awe of that power, the power to transform, should I have the courage to live the lesson. Saturn is in an aspect of my birth chart that indicates accelerated growth. Yep, I can definitely appreciate that. Saturn is also in my daughter's chart, in a similar aspect. We have come into this world as a team, to learn and grow together. For her, it may be a bitter pill to swallow. To know that you have asked for this life… it must be hard to take. But I hope she can be grateful that she has chosen a most faithful supporter in me, as her mum. I cannot live her life but I can help her to do it, to give her the tools to navigate her path as well as she can. We all have a hand to play, we just play the best game we can, with the cards we are given. That is what I feel I have been doing, playing my hand.

I've reached a point, which you might consider according to the philosophy of yoga, where I am less affected by the play of the gunas. I see the play now. I used to see the opposites, especially keenly after my daughter was ill, but now I see them at play more from a distance and I think 'oh, that is just that' and I am not so concerned by it. It is just the play of things, I don't have to let it affect me, if I don't want it to. I have a choice. I am not now so driven by my feelings and impulses. There's a peace and a clarity. An acceptance. I guess, the story is how I got to this place.

Devastated

There can be defining moments in our lifetime. My daughter's illness and subsequent disablement was one of them.

I used to think, in arrogance, that nothing could faze me. I had not ever been presented with an experience that I could not handle. It's not that I was overly confident, just simply that I had never felt overly stretched in any direction.

But that changed on 25th September 2006, when my daughter was 23 months old. On that day I called NHS Direct, was told that Poppy should urgently see a doctor, and was subsequently taken by ambulance to hospital. Little did I know then that this would be the start of a seven and a half week stay (eight days of those in paediatric intensive care) and within a few days, my daughter would be so close to death that a doctor remarked a few months later: 'We didn't know she was going to make the weekend."

I would only make it home for 24 hours each week, just long enough to eat non-processed food, wash some clothes and gym binge. I would stay either on the ward or at a close-by charitable house. I would drink a couple of glasses of wine, just to get to sleep each night. I would spend all my waking hours with my daughter, slipping into the spiritless hospital routine of eternal waiting – waiting for rounds, waiting for blood to be taken and so on. As soon as I awoke, I'd race back to the ward to spend all day in the draining heat of the ward until she had gotten to sleep at night. It was relentless and that was just how it affected me, let alone what my girl went through. She was the protagonist; I was merely a supporting character.

I have just looked through some photos that I took during that time period. At the time, I felt it was somehow important to document some of this experience. Perhaps I had an intuition that these would be the defining moments of our lives, well at least of my life. It's actually a few days after the anniversary of Poppy's stroke, as I write. Sometimes I remember, sometimes it goes by without my marking it. Today I have wept like I used to, looking at the pictures pre-stroke of Poppy helping her Dad wash his van. No trousers on, wearing welly boots and a plastic apron, playing with the hose, not really helping Dad at all, simply enjoying the experience of watering the tarmac. Or standing in our lounge, PJ's still on, trying on Daddy's flippers even though they are gigantic compared to little her.

Then a few days later, in intensive care, tubes coming out of her face,

arms, groin, unconscious, unaware, sedated. I weep. I remember. I remember the hopelessness. I could do nothing. I could only witness. All I could do was take each day at a time, trying to get through this one to see another one unfold before me as if it was a surreal dream. To hope beyond everything else I held dear, that my girl would make it through. I would have given up everything I had, to have taken her place, for this to not have been happening to her. I would have made a deal with the devil himself to save her from this experience – I remember feeling that so strongly. To protect her. But I could do nothing.

What a very profound lesson in the presence of a higher power. A power beyond anything I could comprehend or influence. A power beyond me. A power that made me feel desperately weak, empty, hopeless and broken. I felt broken by the experience. I had lost my way. I had become undone. I was so thoroughly sad, and that sadness at times over the years was almost too much to bear. But bear it I did, because there was no other option. Our pain and sadness cannot be taken away. It is ours to hold or keep or express, our choice how we process that grief, that sadness, that loss. I felt I had lost so much, and I was wandering in a void of utter hopelessness and overwhelm.

I can't say I felt lonely. I was alone in this experience, which of course only I could know, since it is my experience, my story. Only

I can experience my story as it is. Only I will ever understand what I felt and what I thought, the vast width and breadth of it, how my experience of what life could be and bring exponentially expanded beyond what I could ever have imagined. That is the way of it. I don't expect anyone to truly understand, that is the nature of our human experience. We are alone, but I feel that means we can appreciate the times when we are met with understanding and compassion by others. What a gift, to meet someone, outside of ourselves, who has a glimmer of understanding, if even for a moment, however fleeting.

Poppy and I originally were taken by ambulance on a Monday to Bath Royal United Hospital, but were transferred to the Bristol Royal

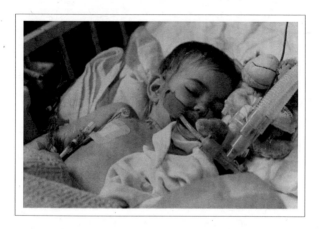

Hospital for Children shortly after. By Wednesday of the same week, she had been diagnosed with E-coli infection and as a result was experiencing the effects of Haemolytic Uraemic Syndrome (HUS). I'd never heard of it. In the evening rounds, I was compelled to ask a question I did not want to know the answer to: could she die? The answer was: "We won't let that happen." So, that is a yes, I thought...

My dad came to visit with Hilary, his partner, the following day, Thursday. Should he continue with the planned trip to Australia, leaving the following day to visit my brother, taking his grand-daughter with him to see her father? As I understand it, he agonised over the decision. At that time, Poppy was scheduled to have some straightforward-sounding surgery the next day, surgery that would do the job of her kidneys, which were not working. My dad made the decision to go. It must have been a difficult call to make. Hilary told me some time later that when he left us that evening, my dad cried. They departed for down under early the following morning.

But later that day, on the Friday, Poppy's bowel started to prolapse. Straightforward-sounding surgery became a little bit more complex and numerous. 'Risk of death' was added to the consent forms. I can only summarise my feelings with: WTF? Later that afternoon, Paul (her dad) and I watched as Poppy's pain increased and her body slowly slumped further into the mattress of her cot. We were told to look out for 'brain involvement'. I didn't really comprehend what that meant but I believe I found out.

Those hours were agonising, waiting for Poppy's surgery slot. It was tortuously uncomfortable watching her suffer. You'd do almost anything to make it stop, but again, my own inadequacy on that point, I have already outlined.

Around 30 minutes before she was called for surgery, Poppy suddenly raised her head from the fixed position she had been in all afternoon, and let out a deep, slow gasp. I now believe this could have been the moment the blood vessel burst in her brain, but I can't be sure.

To our intense relief, the anaesthetist finally came for Poppy. The main renal consultant joined us shortly after and shared with us that she was acutely worried about Poppy's condition. That indicated to me the situation had progressed from WTF to WTFx10. It's difficult to quantify.

Only one of us could go with Poppy into the anaesthetic room, and I went. Tears even now arise as I recall whispering to my daughter that I would see her later in the recovery room. That was what I uttered, but in my head, I said goodbye to her. I didn't know if I was going to see her again. But I had to leave her hearing the certainty of her outcome, whatever I might have said to myself, I felt she had to hear the conclusion would be positive, however dubious I actually felt. I cannot really express in words what that was like. Something profound occurred. A deep vacuous place had been discovered, an emptiness so vast and wide it was incomprehensible. I had never known it was there. I had discovered my arrogance and it was pretty epic.

Waiting to find out if I would see my girl again were fathomless hours. I cannot quite put into words how I felt. But what may have been theoretical up to that point – what it would be like to lose a child – started to take shape and form. How would I live, how could I be without her? Like a picture I was slowly painting, the fine details were being added and colour made it vivid. Those few hours changed me in a way I cannot quite articulate. I realise now when I read author Philip Pullman's description of a person being separated from their daemon, why that resonates with me. I could feel that deep-wrenching separation, I could see what it looked like and although I did not lose Poppy, although she did not die, just the fact that I began to paint that picture, that it began to have substance, touched me in such a deep place that I am not sure I will ever forget the feeling.

Had she died, a part of myself so visceral and vulnerable would have been touched – in fact, it had been touched during those few hours. Like a part of my soul was being stripped from me. That is what it felt like. That is why I would have given anything, everything in that moment, to not have that happen. My biggest fear could have been realised and I absolutely quantified what I would have done to avoid it. And I know that even though my girl made her way back to the land of the living, had she gone to the land of the dead, either way, I still knew that I would have given everything I had, my very soul, to have her back. Even if she had had to live without me, I would have given myself up to take her place, without a thought, in a second, I would have given all of myself.

What a realisation, one that I cannot un-know. Deeply profound.

To know that it was so much out of my power to have that decision be mine. Of course, I could not influence whether she made it back or not. There was nothing I could do; I was so entirely helpless. I knew what I would give to keep her here, living, but it was not my choice or decision to make, it was entirely beyond my control. A higher power would determine the outcome. All I could do was watch, observe. It was the most peculiar sort of out-of-body experience. To watch it unfold and have so much of myself invested in the outcome. To know so much hung in the balance. Everything. Everything I had, everything I was, everything was hanging in the balance. Would she come back to me?

I was heartbroken.

I don't even recall now how long the surgery took – five, six, seven hours? I do remember after around an hour of my leaving the anaesthetic room, we were told they had managed to stabilise her. Whatever the duration, at some point we were told the surgery was complete and we could see her in the Paediatric Intensive Care Unit (PICU), where Poppy was in an isolation room, connected to a wide array of syringes, sedated, on a ventilator, and being automatically administered pain medication. She was still here.

Sometimes I have felt that it was our love for each other that did keep her here. I had the chance to be a mum, she had the chance to have a mum. We had the chance to be together, to love each other. So much. She is the love of my life.

It was difficult for me to not have my father present at the time. We have always been close. He was to be in Australia for a couple of weeks. Of course, I understood the reason for the absence, but I found it tough nonetheless.

Poppy received around eight days of haemo-filtering (where her blood was whizzed around to separate the different elements to enable plasma replacement), then seemed to recover from the HUS, but it was plainly evident that she had had a stroke and had been affected on one side. Already, even when unconscious, her left arm and leg were noticeably tighter.

I remember the day she was taken off the ventilator. We managed a short cuddle before she began to look uncomfortable and had to be transferred back to the bed. First contact. I cried.

It was difficult for Paul. At some point he had to go back to work. I know he felt conflicted. He'd come to visit every evening, and take over at the weekend. For six days a week, I'd follow a dysfunctional routine. I needed alcoholic assistance to sleep in order to numb my mind and silence my thoughts, which were scattered, intense and confused. Then get up early, to be back in time for Poppy waking up. Sometimes she would wake during the night, to be comforted by a nurse. I often wondered what she thought. 'Where's Mum?' She may have been frightened. She may have been confused. 'What is happening to me?' It may have been a fearful time.

I felt overwhelmed. Ironically, of course, I didn't really understand quite how my life would change – how both Poppy's and my life had already changed. We can only absorb and comprehend so much at any one time. But I had to step up, even though I was struggling to understand very much at all, or so it seemed that way.

Inevitably, eventually, we were discharged. No doubt, the team supporting Poppy saved her life. However, we were dropped into a vacuum. Out of sheer naivety, I expected more support. I was initially overwhelmed that Physiotherapy and Occupational Therapy were to be demonstrated to me, but that I would deliver it. I alone was carrying the can of responsibility. That was how it felt.

Of course, I threw myself into doing as much as I could. My unuttered expectation was that by the time Poppy started school, she might be not too dissimilar to her peers. That was only one expectation of many that had to be amended, reworked and revised – through much grief, disappointment and sorrow.

But it wasn't just new expectations that were to be amended. I realised I had unconscious expectations that had been spotlighted, so I could witness them surface only to vanish in an instant as if they had never existed at all. I had a lot to adjust from the past and had so many more adjustments ahead of me. What a lesson in letting go. But I didn't realise I had asked for all of this, that this was what my soul chose to learn, this was part of my journey, my evolution. At the time though, and before that realisation, it was a bitter lesson, one which had to be taken again and again. I now see I have learned a little.

For several years, I felt an all-encompassing sorrow and grief. As if I was staring into an abyss without end. I was just so very sad. I didn't feel guilt or blame, just so incredibly sorry. And I could not see any good in where I was. There was no light, respite, refuge or comfort. I felt entirely lost.

The relationship I had with Poppy's father did not survive. We separated when Poppy was three. One of my best friend's described once how she felt I was so strong at the time of Poppy's illness. I'm not sure. I didn't feel strong, in fact I felt my seeming strength had dissipated. As for Paul, we all cope in our own way, that is all. We both coped in our own way, we unravelled together but apart. All I knew is that I gave everything of myself to Poppy. I simply had nothing left. Nothing for Paul anyhow.

When Poppy went to visit her father, I would allow myself to cry. I would allow my heart to break, expressing such deep sorrow, I could only truly express it alone. I felt so sorry for Poppy. I also felt sorry for myself.

I remember a friend asking me if I was torturing myself, by running events through and round my head again and again. I now appreciate that I was processing. I am so grateful that I cried and cried until I could no more. Having practiced yoga for some years now, I have come to understand that I cannot divert, hide from or mask my pain. It is my responsibility to experience every single bitter-sweet expression because then healing can begin, moving towards acceptance and eventually towards gratitude. Not that I claim to have eradicated pain. Simply that I know what it is and that I can choose to express it, or not. For me now, pain and suffering is a state of mind. It is possible for it to be present but not so very present at the same time. It's there, but not like a fog before my eyes. It doesn't have to be everything I see and everywhere I look. It can be a far-off place. I've been there, but it's my choice to visit again. For some years though, my pain was all I could see and everywhere I looked. I had many moments of intense self-pity. I could see nothing other than my own pain. It was a sorry place to be for sure.

It was a good couple of years before I could talk about Poppy's illness without bursting into tears whilst doing so. It was several more before I could even contemplate any sort of acceptance and more still before that seed of acceptance sprouted into something sustainable. It takes time. I believe we all go at our own pace.

So, I was in a very different place then. A place before understanding that I had gotten exactly what I had asked for. That everything was exactly how it was meant to be, in all its wonderful technicolour pain and beauty.

Being rebuilt

When I was young, maybe six, I remember lying in bed and wondering what would happen when I died. I distinctly remember a cold emptiness gnawing my stomach whenever I thought that this life just, well, ended. That didn't seem right. What about all the love I felt, that couldn't just end? That love could not be for nothing, could it? And if we only had one life, then we could live selfishly with no consequence. I didn't then know what was the answer, but now I realise I was contemplating the concept of reincarnation and karma.

After Poppy was ill, I lost my confidence. It took a while for me to work out quite what in. I lost confidence in myself. In my ability to cope, my ability to manage. I was lost. I lost my way. I know I acted on occasion out of character, out of what you might call my 'true self'. I did some things I am not proud of. Some were rather extreme knee-jerk reactions, for me anyway. They were mainly connected to feeling constricted, restrained. Something would splurge out, it had to be released. I realise now it was all just events, just stuff. I can't over-analyse. I simply needed to accept what happened and focus on understanding what was activated behind the action, and deal with that. I don't very often 'act out' anymore. I have learned self-restraint, through outward restraint. Seeking freedom outside of myself has never satisfied me, so I learned to seek freedom inside. The only freedom we can experience, I feel. Anything else is temporary and transitory. It does not satiate.

For years, I felt broken, like I didn't function properly, like I was defective. I realise I was being dismantled. All my unconscious wishes and dreams were peeled from me, so I could start again from scratch. In the beginning, it felt raw and the wound was tender, but slowly I rebuilt myself. I am still rebuilding myself. I now see it as a process that doesn't end. But I take part in that rebuilding. I am an active participant. I am making my Self. I am building a life of which I am proud and which sits in alignment with my core beliefs, in a way I didn't even think about before my daughter was ill. What is my true purpose? I think I am nearer to understanding what that is.

How did I come to accept my situation? It wasn't a sudden occurrence and I am sure I have a way to go. I got tired of it, I think. I had cried enough, felt enough pain and suffered enough. I really think that was it. It just was not sustainable; I couldn't carry it around any longer. I had to let it go, I had to move on.

Yoga really helped. I gained a life-long and supportive friend when

I discovered yoga. I now have a place to go for refuge and release. I am not meaning to advocate to everyone the benefits of yoga, but I think finding some way of tapping into our own inner resources (as my dad would say, digging deep) is the key to coping, managing, accepting and ultimately growing. I feel I have support behind me. I have my deities to whom I chant every morning. They are cheering me on. Pushing me to be more, give more, love more, to see the beauty in everything and everyone. To be, and be grateful. I am exactly where I am meant to be, and everything is exactly the way it is meant to be. It is absolutely perfect, every single sublime moment. We are all perfect imperfections. What a relief to know it!

My life as a parent carer really showed me what was important. It's not what we are led to believe or sold in the paper, in popular media or advertisements. What is important is our love and connection to others. To be in a situation where you never really move too far away from the fundamentals of life (urine, poo and vomit) is a blessing. I don't get too caught up in what I look like, how I might appear to others, what others think of me, all those things I might feel I need to prove or feel insecure about. I have nothing to prove. I have nothing to feel ashamed of. As long as I do right by my girl, I am on the right track. She is such a ray of pure light and love. She really does deserve my unconditional love and respect. Why would I not give her all that I have? To know she is loved, every part of her. All her perfect imperfections. If we all felt that unconditional love, what a different world this could be.

I have often felt we live in a bubble, Poppy and I. Our world makes sense. It is when we go outside that it's a bit screwy. We know what it is really about. I once read a book, a very lyrical portrayal of a mother's first few years making sense of her life with her disabled child. At one point, she described her life like being in a room, watching the world happen outside the window, watching the world go about its business. That really struck a chord with me. There is a sense that the world happens, it goes on. And for me, the life I share with Poppy is separate in the sense that we don't fit the agreed norms of society, in many ways. But that isn't necessarily a negative thing. We are a little bubble of love, me and my girl. We make sense. But there is a separation between us and most of the outside world. I now fully accept that and embrace it. I am not trying to conform. I don't feel upset when we are stared at (that doesn't mean that I would prefer us not to be) but I accept the world as it is. Otherwise I might feel like I continually have to fight something or prove something or be something. We can just be. The outside world can just be too. That is not to say that I don't care, simply that I feel I know what I choose to care about. What I care about is conveying to my daughter that she is completely loved for exactly who she is. I accept I cannot live her life for her, that I can only help her to build the skills she might need to live her life, a life that I am sure will be extraordinary. The life of a parent carer and that of their disabled child is extraordinary.

During my yoga teacher training, I was encouraged to begin a personal practice, which has transformed my life. I have slowly increased the practice to every day. I now do something daily and it really provides an anchor. Yoga is a safe-haven for me. Tapping into internal resources has enabled me to stay stable. I have developed my ability to discern, and develop my energy resources. Yoga has enabled me to tap into unlimited energy, and that energy and ability to focus really helped me to get through the Special Educational Needs and Disability (SEND) tribunal.

Staying steady

Throughout the tribunal process, I was very aware of the need to stay steady. I needed to set my intention and hold it, to not waver or deviate from that course. That was how I felt about it. Like steering a yacht, I had to set my sights on the horizon, and keep the rudder pointing in that direction, regardless of the conditions – and by grace, we would get there.

It was a Physiotherapist that one day mentioned, off-hand, that she had always wanted to work at a school in Hampshire for physically disabled young people. I believe her comment wasn't made for us to take forward necessarily, but that is what I did. I researched the school and from what I saw, I discussed with Poppy the idea of taking a look. Poppy and I went to the Open Day in the Spring Term. Poppy was resistant because she had already decided in her head that she was too able to go there. So she proved that by insisting on walking around the whole school, which exhausted her. Indeed, she proved her point.

I went with an open mind. Could this solve the school conundrum that we had been having since Poppy was about seven or eight? I didn't have a crystal ball but our experience of mainstream school had indicated to me that things could prove increasingly rough for us. This was compounded when Poppy started Secondary School. Around the same time, I started working for charity HemiHelp, who support young people with Hemiplegia and their families. I attended some training in Bristol about brain injury and it was a revelation. It was the most influential information I had received up to that point. It explained why Poppy could forget things that only happened yesterday. It explained why she could be stubborn and have a fixed mind-set. Clearly there were many aspects of brain injury that I had become aware of as Poppy grew and matured. Yet, from a medical perspective, professionals only really ever concentrated on the physical aspects, not any cognitive. The proverbial penny dropped.

But as that penny dropped my expectation of school changed. Poppy's cognitive needs must be met. And equally importantly, I gave Poppy a goddamned break. I reset my expectations of her. I no longer expected her to remember anything. Yes, anything. That's not to say that she cannot remember anything, just that I can't expect her to remember everything (which is true of everyone in reality, including me). Of course, she does remember an awful lot, she is learning, but I no longer get frustrated if she does not. If she remembers, great – if not then we move on and I provide her with support. Learning about how a brain injury also impacts upon processing speed, concentration and executive function (those are the main areas along with memory) meant I revised many expectations of Poppy and therefore our relationship became more harmonious and aligned. Now I can offer strategies or scaffolding to help Poppy, rather than criticise or become frustrated or even angry. I'm not perfect, I know I've directed those towards Poppy in the past. But now I had the knowledge to support not doing that. However, it also meant that really I expected those working closely with Poppy to step up too.

When I first told Poppy's mainstream school that I was applying to the Local Authority for change of placement, it brought up some interesting attitudes. A professional reminded me that it was 'public money I was talking about'. Quite right. I take that very seriously, but I have a right to campaign for what I think is right for my child. Especially when my child is now regularly talking of self-harming or wishing she were dead, as a result (I felt) of a lack of support and a lack of understanding of her individual needs. Over the years, I have come to realise that I refer to my own internal authority. I do of course refer outside of myself to check that what I am thinking is reasonable. I have trusted experts for that, but if I feel something is worth pursuing, I will on my own authority.

That initial meeting was the beginning, the first step in many steps towards our ultimate goal of getting Poppy enrolled in this alternative school. It was a course that I was wholly prepared for. I set realistic expectations. The Local Authority would refuse, which they did. No surprise then, no disappointment, just the path I had anticipated. So, it was actually going exactly to plan. For reasons I will not go into here, I asked the Local Authority, due to an administration error, to consider for a second time. Of course, the answer was no; the current provision could meet Poppy's needs. Still, on my anticipated track then. From there, I made the application to the tribunal. I was very lucky that I qualified for Legal Aid. I did get support. There were many twists and turns, the tribunal was delayed, cancelled, rescheduled, almost cancelled again, but finally we were going to tribunal...

I didn't really want to put Poppy through attending, but I felt it was critical that the panel witness for themselves the difficulties Poppy experienced or they might never truly understand. How can you get a handle on somebody by reading a report, however well written? This had been a block in the past, I felt. After all, from a medical 'on paper' perspective, Poppy should be a more able, simpler case. She needed to come to the tribunal, and the stress incurred would just have to be weathered.

The panel needed to hear from Poppy herself – after all, this decision was about her, her well-being and her future. Due to the difficulties she experiences as a result of her brain injury, being put on the spot and having to answer questions from strangers, especially in such a loaded, formal situation, I suggested that Poppy prepare something to read out. She could write something in her own words, describe her experience from her perspective, and then practice it in the lead up, so she could be in the best position to read it aloud on the day.

We prepared using strategies that I had learned during some brain injury training. Poppy told me all the things that she found difficult and why she felt that was so, as well as her aspirations for the future and how mainstream school would not get her there, where she wanted to be. She also talked about what she felt the proposed school could provide, from the many visits we had made there, and the overnight stay and day in class, which formed part of the application process. I arranged these on post-it notes and then we grouped them together, all those of a shared theme – physical (getting around school), social (making and keeping friends), in class (academic) and anything else that came up. Then, we took them one by one and I typed as Poppy spoke about her experience, what she really felt, why she wanted to make this huge and significant change.

On the day, Poppy's appeal was provided to the panel in advance, just in case Poppy was not able to read it out. Poppy was given the opportunity to read her appeal first, with minimal adults in the room, so as to limit how intimidated she might feel. She was reluctant, I could see. I quietly reminded her that she could refuse, but that if she could read it out, in her words, with her own voice, this would have the most impact. She mustered the courage to read it out. She did an amazing job, reading slowly and clearly as we had practiced. What pluck.

The aim is to have only one tribunal session – we actually needed another and even then, the closing statements had to be submitted by email. I made sure that I spoke before we left on that final day. I had to leave them with my true feelings, that Poppy had to make this change to ensure she reached her potential on all levels: physical, intellectual, social and emotional. Mainstream school was disabling. Treloar would be enabling.

On reflection, I found the tribunal process incredible. I was in awe. I am not intending that to be wholly positive. I was astounded by many of the arguments. It was a meandering path, and lots more paperwork checking than I had imagined. Thank you Legal Aid, I am not sure how I would have managed without them, and I flatter myself that I am fairly savvy.

Of course I had prepared myself fully, not just expecting the initial refusals and inevitable delays, but I had planned my strategy. In the past, in my formal work, I have shared with other parent carers my understanding that you need to know the game you are playing, otherwise how are you to play the game effectively? Well, I knew this game was the game of evidence. As soon as I informed the Local Authority of my intentions, I began to contact every professional involved in Poppy's care. I asked them to write a letter of support. Some had to be chased and repeatedly reminded. I could do that. I have never been concerned with being liked, and I wasn't going to start now. This was important and I would do what it took, regardless of what others might think of me.

Understandably, professionals could not state that Treloar was the right school for Poppy, that was beyond their remit but they could state her needs and detail the type of support that could meet that need. That was what mainstream school would be measured against. It also meant the Local Authority would have difficulty calling any professional already involved in Poppy's care, as a witness. That was a strength. Their witnesses could only talk in general terms since they had little or no experiential knowledge of Poppy and her difficulties. None could really speak with any real authority. That was a strength. I had learned over the years that you do not give anyone a chance to say no. You provide all the evidence and make your arguments clean and clear, so the only decision that can be made is the one in your favour. You cover all your bases, you look at every angle, you make your play, and you play the game well. That is what I planned, and that is what I did.

I know I can be a formidable opponent. I will observe the game, learn the rules of that game. I will come up with a strategy and I will play to win. After all, I had so much to play for. I had the fate of my child's future for motivation. I had to play to win, I had to be victorious. That is not to say that after all the tribunal sessions, I could determine or predict the outcome. I didn't go too far down the line with my thought process, because I had to focus on a successful outcome, but I had ventured enough to explore my next steps if we were unsuccessful. Step one, withdraw Poppy from school. Step two, appeal.

But it had to go our way, it was the only option – that was how I really felt about it. We had tried a different primary school, we had tried secondary school, we had tried flexi-schooling, we had tried home schooling, we had considered alternative Steiner schooling. I could not be stretched any more and neither could Poppy. Something had to give, and it could not have been either of us. As if we had been ring-fenced a long time ago, and that fence kept moving, making our enclosure smaller and smaller, until there was nowhere left for us to go, we could not be squeezed any more. We had gotten to breaking point. I think to many, the application to change schools was an extreme measure, and I fully understood how unlikely it was that we would achieve our aim. To make the step from one school to another is big; to make the step from mainstream to a special school is huge; but to leap-frog straight to a residential special school, well it was explained to me that was singularly uncommon. It may have been a remote chance, but it had to be. We had exhausted all our options and this really was the only viable alternative.

Even those changes of school that were made, I still had serious doubts they would succeed. Until we discovered Treloar School, I had not considered that any of them could work. Treloar School could work. Not ideal, because you have to be realistic, but a much, much closer fit than any other. So, we were reaching for the stars in some respect. We were aiming high, but in doing so, it would solve many problems in one go – the question of supporting independence into adulthood, the question of appropriate support in class so that Poppy had half a chance of achieving her academic potential, the chance to receive regular therapeutic input, the chance to receive regular mental health support, the chance to access services we had never received before, the chance to build friendships, the chance to meaningfully compete, the chance to begin to experience some success. The chance to finally expand.

At the time, could Poppy have gotten any lower, could she have felt any more isolated, despondent and hopeless? For about a year, every day during my morning ritual, I asked for a succinct verdict: for the tribunal to find the only school that could meet Poppy's needs was Treloar. That could be the only outcome, and the whole universe in a sense was in support, or so I had to believe. I had to trust; I could not waver. I had to stay steady and by sheer force of will, that is what I did, and by the grace of God, that was decided. When I received the call from Legal Aid informing me that our appeal had been successful, I cried – not immediately, but it came. I was so relieved. I was so pleased for Poppy. Now she could see out her last few weeks at mainstream school knowing they would be her last. That would keep her going.

And I finally felt hopeful, that perhaps this was a turning point. We had reached a junction, and one path simply could not be walked. There was only one way forward and that was finally upwards and onwards. It was an immense achievement. We had done it! The universe had answered our plea, with a resounding vote of confidence.

I knew this decision would signify a momentous change for us both.

Responsibility

To know what one is responsible for... I am responsible for my feelings, my thoughts and my actions. Just me, no-one else. If I take responsibility for myself, truly, then I have no justification to blame anyone else. I am the writer of my own destiny.

I have spent considerable time thinking and considering my responsibility. As a parent carer, I think you can easily be sucked into feeling responsible for almost anything or everything, but is that realistic and is it sustainable? As a parent, you take responsibility for your young person. Most of us want to do it, because of the bond of love that binds you to your child, and their inherent vulnerability and lack of capacity. But what if caring for your young person denotes extra responsibilities? What if your life with your young person does not follow the more normal flow of development? What if your young person does not reach those more regular milestones like being able to dress themselves, feed themselves, go to the toilet by themselves? Then of course the parent will step up to provide that support while it is needed. Sometimes that need does not go away. It remains your responsibility.

So, I have felt it of utmost importance to determine what is and is not my responsibility. Of course, there will exist an overlap because not one of us exists in isolation. But what really is my responsibility? At the very basic level, I know I can only ever be fully responsible for what I feel, what I think and how I act (this relates to the Cognitive Behavioural Therapy model, which I have worked with formally with counsellors and informally on my own with various books). It does share some theory with yoga, I feel. The aim of yoga is self-development, to realise the truth of reality. One truth of reality is that I am only responsible for my Self; what I feel, what I think and what I do. Therefore, I can never be responsible for how anyone else feels, thinks or acts – in fact, that is their responsibility. They are ultimately responsible for their growth and development. There is some freedom in that realisation. I am not responsible for everything or everyone, simply for myself.

I feel this with Poppy. I know I am not disabled myself. But I do experience disablement as a result of the situation, which is inevitable and realistic. When Poppy was 11, she experienced repeated focal seizures, sometimes experiencing clusters of 20 or more at a time, at several times of the day. She could not attend school, and this was the situation for around three months. During that time, I was largely house-bound. I rarely went out, I simply could not. I was limited by that situation. It was what it was and I had to get on with it. I did find it extremely limiting and I did feel curtailed and confined, but there was simply nothing I could do – it was beyond my control. But I had to be there, that was my responsibility. There was no-one to help or step in. My break came when Poppy went to her father's.

I have talked about acceptance and I have talked with Poppy about it. I have to accept that she has chosen her path, when she chose this life. I cannot wrap her up in cotton wool, to try to shield her from the world. We have to go out, we may be stared at, we inevitably come into contact with others, that is just the way of it. It is Poppy's responsibility to live her life. It is my responsibility to be her mother, perhaps offering useful skills, providing advice based on my experience, assisting when appropriate, but ultimately, she has to live it. I cannot do that for her. If I tried to take control or responsibility for her living her own life then I would ultimately be robbing her of her chance to step up to her responsibility, to step into her power.

Only when you realise and practice taking responsibility for yourself can you truly take charge of your life, to control what you can (what you feel, what you think and how you act). Otherwise you can become stuck in victimhood or blame. It is all too easy to look outside of yourself for excuses about why something has happened or turned out the way it has, instead of searching internally for the answer, and taking responsibility for your choices. Life can very quickly feel out of control if you do not take on that responsibility, if you choose to cop-out, and it is a choice. It may seem like the easy choice too, but in the long run you are simply cheating yourself of the opportunity to live life your way.

If I did not take responsibility for myself, I could not apologise when I act outside of my internal value system – I might blame some external factor. I didn't get enough sleep, so I am grumpy. Maybe a shop assistant was rude to me, so I snap at you, because I am ticked off. We can make so many excuses for our behaviour when often, we simply need to take a good hard look in the mirror to see the answer. I know I do not always act with honour, or grace, or calmness, or compassion, but if I notice I have, I do try to apologise and do it as soon as I've noticed. I try to act with integrity. I am not perfect and I may not always act perfectly but I will apologise if I feel I have not taken responsibility for myself, if I have acted out of character or out of my integrity, and I will try to do better.

Through taking responsibility for myself, for understanding I am only ever really accountable to myself, then I can slowly reduce relying on others or paying too much attention to anyone else's opinion. Again, of course, we do not exist in isolation, but to a large degree I am confident that I am my own best counsel. This has been so helpful over the years since I have come into contact with many external voices, sometimes with conflicting viewpoints. For several years, Poppy had around 40 hospital appointments per year. That results in a lot of information to process. I discovered a skill in myself… and in part, I thank my mother and father for not providing me with a great deal of guidance growing up – that might be considered a negative, but for me it resulted in my realising at a young age that I had to 'step up' and take responsibility for my own choices, for which I am grateful. The skill I discovered that I had developed was the ability to listen very carefully to what I was being told, to all the different opinions, but importantly, then I would go away and filter that information – to think, to research, to make enquiry and over time to discover what I really felt.

Sometimes what I felt or thought was in line with a professional, sometimes not. If it was not then I would, to some degree, make my case. Why did I disagree? Sometimes, it meant that I needed to recruit help, especially if it meant I needed to argue against a professional's opinion to access a service for Poppy. In some instances, at key times, I first measured my intended response with a trusted advisor. Thankfully I have been supported by many people whom I have come to trust to provide me with a measured opinion, drawing on their particular and individual experience and expertise, which I might lack. I would check in with those trusted advisors to ensure I was feeling or thinking reasonably. Partly because you have to choose your battles, but also because you have to be reasonable when resources are at a premium. That said, I would still pursue something if I felt it absolutely necessary for Poppy's well-being. Nonetheless, generally speaking, once I had determined what I really thought, then I would pursue my goal with confidence and intent. I could fully take responsibility for that action, and I would follow it through to its conclusion, perhaps drawing on any evidence to argue the case for Poppy. That might involve recruiting a different professional to back me up. Whatever it took. I could challenge an opinion because I took responsibility for myself and knew I could only ever be accountable to myself. I can respect another's opinion but I do not necessarily need to make it mine, be guided by it or limited by it.

I am very grateful to my mother. She may not have necessarily provided me with the most stable or regular of upbringings. I witnessed many outbursts of misdirected rage, which provided me with ample opportunity to consider responsibility. Having been the target (not that I was the only one in my family, she was fair and spread it around) of that misdirected rage, I know it is very unpleasant, painful and upsetting. Having had that experience, I felt the confusion and dismay, the downright injustice, of being blamed or somehow made accountable for something that wasn't my fault – in actual fact, at its core, it was something I wasn't even alive for; it was an event that left my mother feeling alone, abandoned and unloved, at a very young age. I knew, very deeply in my being, that it was not my fault and I could not be made responsible for it, however hard she tried or convinced she was. She had to be responsible for it, since only she could. Now this process took years, of course, these dawning realisations can take years. Especially when it is your parent, a person you inherently trust and believe. It is difficult to step outside of your conditioning, to dare to believe that perhaps your parent could be flawed. Just like me, in fact.

I have received counselling in the past. One session was particularly noteworthy. It allowed me to step out of my past, to step towards a future unimpeded by a responsibility I felt towards my mother. I was asked to close my eyes and remember a pleasant recollection of my mother. I could not really think of anything to be honest at the time (which I am sure is not a true reflection of reality) but at that particular moment, that was how I felt. So, I was asked to conjure a potent memory. I fixed on a recurrently charged one: my mother rowing with my father in the kitchen. On many occasions, I had been drawn into the argument by simply making my physical presence known (you had to walk past the kitchen door to get to the bathroom). That could be enough for my mother to divert her frustration and rage from my father to me. I vividly remember the words: "And you…" Followed by a comprehensively extensive onslaught of my recent misdemeanours and character failings.

I was asked by the counsellor, what is happening? In that moment I was in that kitchen, being thoroughly assassinated by word. The counsellor continued to prompt me: "What is happening now?" At some point, I decided to leave the room and shut the door. It was significant. My physical removal and shutting of the door was my metaphorical way of shutting my mother in with what I believed was her responsibility. Her responsibility to process her hurt, her pain and the rage she felt. It was not mine, so I shut the door to it. Once I shut the door in that counselling session, the responsibility I felt towards my mother, or what was directed towards me, failed to impact my life so much, I was free to simply take responsibility for just myself. It was a significant turning point, and a very important learning experience.

It helped me to navigate the situation I am in now. I am so grateful for that. That I have been provided with the experiences I needed to build the skills that I can now draw upon. I had been given exactly what I needed. What a blessing.

Becoming more precise about my responsibility was important, otherwise I might take on the responsibility of others and accumulate that with my grief. I feel I can only grieve my apparent losses. I cannot grieve for Poppy's too. She has a responsibility to grieve for herself, otherwise she might never do it. If I did take on that responsibility, I might limit her and hold her back from her potential – and what potential she has, to learn and grow. Painful may be the process, but abundantly rewarding, if you have the courage to do it.

Patience

I have not mentioned the more continual grieving that has become an integral part of my journey as a parent carer. All the bitter-sweet moments that are opportunities to grieve just a little more. Sports day, watching Poppy fast-walk the running race, knowing she will be last and by a long way. Bitter-sweet. I felt so proud and so sad at the same time. The opposites again, they keep arising. Watching her being pushed in her wheelchair around a shopping centre by a friend. Bitter-sweet. So pleased she is getting some girly time, but so sad she has to rely on that friend to push her around, in order to experience some independence from me. So much to grieve. I had to develop patience. Patience with myself, and trust that I could work through it.

Interacting with statutory services takes patience. I'd love to know how long we have spent waiting for appointments – we've probably clocked up some hours. We became professional waiters. There is an immeasurable amount of waiting to be done. We go prepared: books, cards, puzzles. We are so patient; it is now noticeable how impatient others can be. It amuses me how you can be standing in a line and the person behind stands just that little bit too close, because they feel as if they are that bit closer to the front of the line because they are physically closer. There are still the same number of people between them and the front of the queue, but still, they choose to stand at your heels. We can play so many mind-tricks on ourselves. Now I can see more clearly what they are. I hope I see my own a little clearer.

Since learning more about how brain injury can affect a person, I have become more patient with Poppy. Not just in obvious ways, like providing more thinking time, for example, but when Poppy is feeling emotional. It has brought us closer. I give her a lot of my time. Time for her to talk and off-load or express how she feels about something that is bothering her, that might take her longer to process, including feelings. In a book I once read about being an adult in a relationship, one thing that resonated was the identification of key moments to create and foster intimacy within our relationships. There might be a time that we know our loved one needs some support but we might feel for whatever reason that we do not have the time, space or capacity to deal with the situation. If we refuse the opportunity to connect and support one another, we lose a chance to be intimate. Reading that made a difference to my availability to Poppy. I now make every effort to notice those opportunities and to take the time to be there for her. It has brought us ever closer. It does take time, but I now realise it is time very well spent. I have exercised patience with her, providing her a safe space, I hope, to express herself and not feel hurried or judged. We have all the time in the world.

I have learned to be patient with myself. Learning that what I am going through is a process which takes as long as it takes. Clearing trauma takes time. It also has taken considerable effort. I now view grief, as well as depression, as a process. There are stages and they are worked through and one thing becomes another. There is transformation. Now that I see it more as a process rather than identifying so closely and intimately with the actual feelings or thoughts that arise, I am not so attached to them, and am far less concerned by them. Now I can label that feeling or that thought, or that process and see it for what it is, and be far less affected by it. As if it loses its power as soon as I label it. As soon as I see it for what it is, its hold over me effortlessly falls away. Ultimately, I suffer less. That is such a relief. I am more free to be.

I am much more patient with others. We all experience pain, we all suffer. What may seem trifling to one may be everything to another. It seems to me to depend on our perspective. I used to be a little less patient – after all, I was cornering the market in self-pity. Over time though, I came to appreciate that what might seem petty from my perspective can still have a significant impact on another, from their perspective. I can still exercise compassion. What is important to us is important to us, whether someone else understands it or not. There is a perception of importance, that is the point.

In many respects I feel like I had to develop patience, it was inevitable. What would be the cost if I did not? I might continually feel annoyance or irritation. Where might that have led? I have felt those emotions and they are not gratifying to experience, especially over time. I might become consumed by them. I chose to develop patience – a sustainable and healthy option. For peace of mind, it was perhaps the only option.

However, waiting for services or decisions or whatever, while Poppy was suffering – that took some mastery, and still does. Waiting for the tribunal process to take its course while Poppy was attending school, watching her self-confidence and self-esteem slowly erode. That was hard, and if it was hard to watch, what must it have been like for Poppy? There have been some agonising periods. All I could do was be patient and try to get Poppy through those tough patches. During those last few weeks at secondary school, Poppy received a Lego Minifigure of her choice from myself, in return for every week she completed. A small gesture it may have been, but it contributed to her getting by. It got us both through. We did what we had to do to get by.

I remember I was upset once – it must have been a few years after Poppy was ill – and a family member asked: "Why don't you get over it?" At the time, I felt I could not just get over something so pivotal and central in my life, let alone something that was ever-present and all-consuming. After all, Poppy's difficulties did not just evaporate and therefore, the frightful situation I was in could not disappear either. What may have sat behind that question was a sense of not wanting to watch me suffer. It could also have been the fatigue that I have often felt from others. A sort of 'oh blimey, not this again...!' I think there can be fatigue when it comes to other people's trauma – you just cannot bear to hear another person's misfortune one more time. I can understand that. Yet for the person expressing sadness or grief, it is still present. My story was a record that was stuck – I knew that, but I could not at that time break out of the cycle. Partially because, as soon as Poppy went into hospital, I was on support mode and that switch did not turn off.

As Poppy's parent, how could I take time for myself to grieve? How could I not put every tiny bit of energy into supporting her day after day? I had to be on it, I could not take my foot off the throttle. The reality was, of course, that I did show emotion from time to time, but on the whole, I tried to shield my own grieving from her. She had enough to deal with. That is why it spilled out when Poppy spent time with her father. That was when I would break. In a way, I suppose, that could be why it took as long as it took. It had its own pace, especially when I was holding back most of the time. It was measured, my grief. My grief had its specific time and place, and that was when Poppy was absent. It was at these times that I processed what I felt and what I thought. It was a controlled trickle rather than a flood. Or that was how it seemed to me. How tiring it was to hold back a flood.

I also had to exercise patience with others when they uttered outwardly ridiculous things about my situation. I've heard some perfectly silly statements in my time – all said with good intentions, of that I have no doubt, but in the situation I am in, absurd they are. My top favourite is: "Well, at least she still has one hand." Well, yes, this is factually true, but if you really think through the reality of trying to achieve everything you would normally in life with one hand as opposed to two, you can probably understand my rather astounded (inward) response. When faced with a difficult situation, it is all too easy to try to make things better or offer some solace. Having been on the receiving side, I now opt for listening rather than immediate (although tempting) problem-solving. I go for presence. We are all different (that is undoubtedly true) with different needs and wants, but I try to put the other person first. What do they need from me? Will trying to make things alright in my eyes, really be helping them?

I have harnessed this experience to shape my responses to Poppy if she becomes upset at her situation, which frankly, is to be expected. I can completely understand her frustrations, but I have to admit that I am not her and although I have a unique insight into her situation, I cannot really know what it is like to be her. I listen and I acknowledge her pain, her suffering, her frustration, her anger sometimes. I witness those feelings, all perfectly legitimate of course, because that is all I really can do. I don't have a magic wand and I never will. Eventually, the thoughts or feelings naturally subside and then we can have a more reasonable conversation about what we might actually be able to do to make things better, together as co-authors. It has to come from Poppy – even if I am making suggestions, she can throw them out. But I might offer something of worth or I can help Poppy expand or define something she comes up with. You have to be creative. Thankfully, as a naturally creative person, I have employed that skill in this situation.

I remember a similar event, where I was admitting to my father my doubt that I could cope with the situation I found myself in. Poppy had briefly been discharged, but in reality we were only home a day. Halfway through her hospital stay, she started to experience abdominal pain. It turned out that she was developing adhesions (after abdominal surgery, the intestines can become sticky and form tight loops that painfully trap or block food travelling through the digestive system). Again, that was a term new to me. In the moment when I was expressing my own misgivings, we were home and Poppy was in pain – again. I really couldn't take it, I couldn't be witness to any more pain and suffering. I just couldn't. But I had to and at that moment I confessed my inadequacy. It was difficult because who wants to admit they are sceptical about caring for their own child, especially when that child is in dire need? It was distressing. But my dad said a profound thing, something I have thought back on many, many times. He delivered: "You have to dig deep." He didn't have the answer, but he was pointing to where to find it. I have been digging deep within myself ever since and he was right, of course, we can only ever find our own answers. Someone might point the way, but we have to walk the path. I have to walk my path. Poppy has to walk hers. We might walk together, but ultimately we are responsible for our own path through life, the life we have chosen.

Understanding

Through understanding myself, through trying to understand Poppy, her situation and her difficulties, I have come to have a greater understanding of others.

I make a lot less assumptions than I used to and I feel I am less judgemental. After all, I will only ever really know what I feel or think about anything. Pretty much everything else may as well be considered a guess.

Having a brain injury is quite distinct. It can result in some interesting behaviour and thought processes. Having taken some training and read a few books on the subject, I have come to realise that you cannot really make assumptions about the motives of a person with a brain injury, and if you do, they are normally way off-base. I now understand that if Poppy pauses after being asked a question, it may not be a lack of confidence for her not to reply (as an example), it is more likely that she is simply thinking of an appropriate answer. That might take some time. So, it's no good rushing her – that might just put her under pressure and make it even harder for her to come up with an answer. However, it might also be useful to check that Poppy understood the question, since she can take things quite literally. She might need the question to be tightened up, quantified and made much more specific. It's not much use praising her for her 'good work today' since she might think, 'what good work?', 'what was good about it?', 'what work are you referring to?' I now realise when I talk to Poppy, I am always attempting to quantify and clarify what I say and if I sense there is a gap then I revise as I go along. There is always room for improvement.

I now understand much more intimately the effort that Poppy puts into everyday things. What seems quite simple to me can be quite problematic to her. Like buttons. Or zips. Or walking.

I found it quite impossible to watch the UK Paralympics in 2012 because I cried all the time. To see such courage and determination. To understand how much effort probably went into that athlete competing, whether physically, emotionally, or whatever. It made me cry every time, so I stopped watching it.

To make things easier, without limiting: that is the trick. So many people can dismiss Poppy, to not even ask if she wants to be a part of something, because they have already made an assumption that she could not participate. It has caused much irritation and frustration in the past. To experience limitation and then have that compounded by society's limitations must be, at times, galling to say the least. I try my hardest to avoid doing that. I try to ask the question, to keep things open, to keep opportunity and choice available.

As a disabled person, you can be made to feel useless, worthless and insignificant. I don't mean to make it sound so barren, but those suggestions can sit just under the surface of much of what is done and said. It may not come from a place of prejudice or unkindliness, but it's there nonetheless, quite often.

Poppy has been told so many incredibly ignorant things, I could write a lengthy book about them. As a parent, I have tried my best to counter those views and opinions, whether subtle or more open. That is part of my job as a parent carer, I think. We have had to practice understanding and compassion towards others who simply do not understand. In many respects, how could they?

As I have mentioned, every day I chant a mantra to Bhuvaneshvari, the Goddess of space. Not limited to space, but for what I shared with Poppy one day, space was of relevance. I explained to her that the physical space that she took up, if you drew a line around her and she stepped away, that space, the space she took up, I explained that it was hers. That space was her birthright. That space was sacred, it was created just for her and no-one else, for her to exist in this world. That space could never be taken away from her by the words or deeds of others, however they might try. That Poppy-shaped-space was hers. She could be proud of that space, proud of who she was. In many ways, she had fought to be here, for her space in this world. To be alive, to live. I hope she understood that all the doubters or criticisers, they could not shake her core. There is something deep within us all that is ours, that cannot be touched or marked or affected. It is uniquely us; we are uniquely it. Know that and hold on to it.

Since starting the new school, Poppy has been re-evaluating herself. Now she has the safe space to do so and is receiving more appropriate support, she is consequently working a little less hard to conform and taking a little less time trying to keep up. Poppy can really start to learn to be just herself.

She spent the first year a little hesitantly. That is how I would describe it. Our first summer holiday was frantic. Poppy was quite angry and upset most of the time. I could sense there was an internal struggle going on, which would spill out and normally towards me. She was clearly struggling with something and towards the end of the holiday Poppy was able to articulate what she thought it was. She felt there was a new Poppy trying to emerge, a more confident and prouder version of herself, but her old self was not letting up without a fight.

Poppy told me: "I want to be able to walk into a room and not feel embarrassed or ashamed or have my head down." How remarkable. Poppy started back: a new school year, and a new Poppy. All her teachers have noticed a willingness to be more involved, to contribute and to participate.

I have noticed she is less likely to fall into old habits, which normally express themselves in one of two ways: one, it's my fault (as in me) and two, why is this happening to me? (and then berate me for mostly, on the whole, not knowing the answer!) How remarkable. I feel Poppy is re-forming herself.

We also, over the holiday, looked through the photos from her time in hospital. She had once attempted to view them, but could only manage a couple before having to stop – she could not face them for a reason she could not define. We all process in our own time and space. But this time, we sat together on the sofa and I talked through each photo, providing my history of that time, from my recollection. Poppy also read some brain injury rehabilitation books I had bought a few years ago, which I had found very informative. Poppy had many 'aha!' moments. Ultimately, she understands herself more. Not that she has to feel like she is some sort of weirdo (her words) who can't remember things, for example (which has been one inner critical voice). Instead, it's that she has difficulties most of us experience at some time or another, but she may have to use strategies or scaffolding more often. Her understanding has grown and out of that has come a calm and a peace. Our time together is even more harmonious, now she is fighting herself less often, and that means she is fighting me less often because that is the way it manifests outwardly. Less criticism, less judgement, less 'I should be able to do xxx.' Quite remarkable. Poppy really is quite remarkable, and I applaud her for it.

There may be fluctuations, there always are when we are dealing with inner change, but if we hold our intention, we will get there. I trust she will get there, working towards her acceptance of what is.

To understand, know yourself first.

Stamina

In the words of Ice Cube: "Life ain't a track meet, it's a marathon." I have learned to pace myself.

I used to do more things in a day, plan more and strive for more. I have relaxed that – I had to because I was burning out. My body was exhausted, my mind was scattered and my senses were fried. Plus, it stressed Poppy out to be constantly hurrying and incessantly late. The pace of our lives was driving us both nuts.

Nowadays, at the weekends or during the school holidays, I plan only one thing a day. I allow plenty of time for getting up and getting ready to go out, and that normally includes some Poppy melt-down time. I try to avoid mentioning being 'late' or 'hurrying'. That just doesn't benefit anyone, and it avoids Poppy asking me about a million questions about why we came to be late. This is a much more successful strategy. In fact, trying to act as if we have all the time in the world, even if we do not, is the strategy I strive for. Of course, we may not always succeed but it's a good target.

In fact, the illusion of taking all the time in the world usually makes for a quicker process, whilst hurrying normally results in delays and set-backs. An interesting paradox.

Of course, our pace of life is quite far removed from what might be considered regular. I still rise early, although now that Poppy is at residential school, this means that during the week I can complete any yoga practice during the magical quiet peace of the early morning. I still go to bed at an hour that most would consider indecent, but that is because I am tired. There is still much to organise and manage, even with Poppy at school during the week. Of course, I still manage my time around my commitment to Poppy and her care, and prioritise my time with Poppy at the weekend – I don't want to be doing chores, for example, I want to be spending my time wisely when my girl is home. But my early bird mornings were born out of necessity.

I realised I could only really manage Poppy's care and gruelling morning routine if I was fed, watered and clean before she got up every morning. It was the method that worked for me. I got my quiet time in the early hours of the morning, as opposed to the evening. My preferred routine was back-to-front to everyone else's. So I go to bed at the same time as Poppy, probably when most people are considering their evening relaxation. It does have its draw-backs, inevitably – I am not so able to socialise in the evenings because I am resultantly so tired. A late night for me is 9pm, so I have had to let go of any attachment to a more regular daily pace or routine, and what that might mean for me socially. For me, it has become the lesser of two evils, so I take responsibility for my choices and move on. I may have grieved this in the past, but now I am resolved.

My pace of life is what it is, I have had to accept that my pace is Poppy's pace. We can only go as fast or as far as she can. I had to let go of any aspirations beyond that. I have become very accepting. We get done what we get done. I am grateful for what we do and let go of any disappointment in what we may not. I cultivated a lot of patience along the way. It is astounding what I can get done when I am operating on my own, but I still need to accept the speed I can operate when I am with Poppy. I now have two speeds and I am only really exploring my individual speed again, since Poppy has just recently started attending the residential school. Up to that point, I could only manage one speed. Now I have a little more variety. I cannot deny that the freedom I enjoy when I am on my own is exquisite.

When Poppy started Treloar School, I was very aware of my own pace. There were some things I wanted to get done around the house, such as decorating, that was quite difficult to orchestrate because of time and space restraints. Apart from that, I was very sure I did not want to go filling my time with lots of stuff. I felt like I wanted to merely be for a bit. To take a rest from constantly doing and thinking, to simply being. I had quite clear ideas about the pace I wanted to start at. It was a very odd venture for me. I remember going for a walk in the countryside shortly after Poppy started school, and it was 7.15am when I left the house. I could hardly believe it, that I was out of the house, on my own, at that time in the morning. What a revelation. But I intuitively felt that I shouldn't be intoxicated about the freedom that most take for granted, that I would slowly reintroduce a new time and space for myself. I am still doing that now. I am still pacing myself.

I have felt so utterly overwhelmed in the past with what I felt was on my plate. I felt like I had to do it all. Work, care for Poppy, take care of the house, attend appointments, keep on top of other people's care for Poppy. It was completely bonkers. My life routine was insane.

I still have to be very mindful of what I commit to. I have to accept I live in the real world and my energy can fluctuate and is finite. My primary commitment is to Poppy and always will be. Everything outside of that must be very carefully considered or it can quite quickly lead to overwhelm. I have to admit that my body can still tend towards fight or flight. I am still experiencing trauma, and if I cannot function for whatever reason or on whatever level then can I fulfil my primary commitment? Not really.

What is my life aim? I feel it is to support my daughter, to provide her with the skills she may need to live her life as independently as she can. If I can achieve that then I feel I will have accomplished what I set out to do, whether I was conscious of it or not. Now I feel that this is my conscious life aim.

That means I may have to weather any criticism I might attract, and I have experienced it. I should work full-time, I should not be receiving benefits, I should not blah blah blah – add any number of judgements at this point after the word should... Those types of comments used to bother me a lot, more than they do now, because they dovetailed in nicely with how I felt at the time, when part of me agreed with them on some level. After all, I wasn't doing the job I really wanted, was I? I did not want to be on state benefits, but it was necessary and the alternative was to feel like I was going slowly mad. I was not making choices based on preference, but out of necessity and I wasn't entirely comfortable with that. I felt I was not steering my own ship; it was out of my control. I was in charge of a big, wieldy, careering mess of a life and I was being accused of making the wrong choices, as if I thought I had much of a choice.

At the time, I actually felt there was not much I could do – there was no ideal solution, I could only do the best I could at the time with the information I had available. I had to face imperfection. I had to make the best of it by making decisions and choices that even I perhaps was not that happy about, but they were better than the alternative. What was expected of me, to do it all, to be it all, to be perfect? Who really imposed these standards on me? Myself, of course! They were just reinforced by external voices. I was functioning for some years with contrary beliefs. One belief source originated from thought, another from feeling. My thoughts and feelings were at odds. I thought I should work and achieve; I felt my place was to care for my daughter. Now I think and feel neither. I am inching closer to knowing, which is neither thinking or feeling. Knowing is more accepting. It is what it is. I can only do what I am capable of, whilst holding myself in integrity and in alignment with my core beliefs. That is beyond criticism or judgement, my own or anyone else's.

Even so, in the beginning, that was probably what I was trying to do: to do it all. But it was not sustainable or manageable or even possible. So, my own insecurities were mirrored back to me externally until I woke up and accepted the reality of the situation. I am fallible. I am not perfect. I can only do my best at any one time, with the tools and knowledge I have available. Always to my capacity.

So, I pace myself and try to keep a step back from overwhelm. I do still feel overwhelmed at times, especially when life presents a challenge, which is inevitable. What I try to achieve is a stable core – that way I feel more equipped (internally) to take on the unexpected (external) demands that might arise, which happen continually because that is the way of life. Stuff happens… all the time! How I greet that stuff is really why I am here.

Acceptance

In the beginning, I was lost, completely lost. I didn't know what I was doing or where I was going. My life had just come to a spectacular skidding halt. All I could do was tread water and take every day at a time.

At some point after Poppy's illness, I began having hypnotherapy sessions with a friend, who had recently trained. During this treatment, I remember being asked if anything positive had come of my experience. I could think of nothing. Everything seemed broken and wrong. My daughter, my life as it was. Nothing, nothing about it was positive, all I could see was my own pain and my daughter's pain and suffering.

I was working all the time – I had to because I now had a mortgage. I was working part-time during the hours of school, but before school there was physiotherapy and occupational therapy, and after Poppy had gone to bed, well then, I might do some cleaning or even some freelance work. I was rising at around 5am and sometimes not going to sleep until around 10-11pm. I was exhausted.

When Poppy was at her father's, I would cry and try to catch up on sleep. I was still exhausted. This went on for some time. Living hand to mouth, feeling devastated. Feeling like my life was not my own. It had been taken over by lots of things I came to detest. At times, I felt like I hated my life and considered suicide, something I previously had never felt and never thought I ever would. On top of what I felt was my daughter's suffering was my own suffering, plus my exhausting life. Regular headaches, continual body trembling – my nervous system was overloaded. I was experiencing trauma.

That had to end. Of course, I could not carry on in that way. It may not have ended well. Would I have been hospitalised? At times, I longed to be, just for a goddamned break. What a sorry state to be in. Self-pity is really quite something extraordinary.

Acceptance had to come. It needed to come. It did come, but slowly. It had its own pace, like something outside of myself. I had to wait it out and watch it unfold in its own time and at its own pace. No one could help me do it and I knew there was no saviour to take the pain away (like alcohol, drugs, chocolate, food, partner or any other number of emotional crutches we might choose).

But I could not continue to live in the past – continually feeling 'what if'? And I could not continue to live in the future – continually feeling 'if only'? I had to become present, I had to accept that where I was, that was right where I was meant to be – for all its pain, suffering, beauty and joy. To feel, but not quite so keenly; to grieve, but not so overwhelmingly; to sit within all those feelings, to see them all, to know them all, but not to feel like I have to express them all right now – but equally, the freedom to express them when the time is right. That was where I was moving towards. That is where I am now, although I am not supposing I don't have a way still to go. I now realise evolution and expansion is always happening. But now I know which direction I am going in.

I am not going back. I will not go back to pain and suffering. I know them, and I may more fleetingly visit them at times when I am triggered – anniversaries, family events, hospital appointments – but now I know the feeling or emotion or thought that arises from that, and I more easily see it for what it is. There now does not need to be an automatic reaction, I can now choose whether to express something or act on a thought. I have a choice and choice is freedom. That is not to say that I have become complacent – I might still chase an orthotic appointment, for example. But I need not do it with any frantic quality, or worry about the consequences. I now act with a little more measure, and try to make an appropriate response. That is not to say that I may not adopt some rigorous methods, but I remain open to how things might pan out and I trust more that I will reach my intended destination at some point.

Grieving is a process; I believe it takes its own time. You just have to witness it and importantly, feel every feeling and emotion. Leave nothing unfelt. Eventually, my very immediate suffering and grief ran its course and dried up. There was little left unfelt. I am grateful I did that. How could I move on without feeling every nuance and subtlety? Like I said, I still have moments but they are short-lived, and I now know what I feel and I choose how or if to express it.

In a way, this story is just that: a story. Part of my history and it can be just that: my history. I can see it as a story, it does not have to be quite so personal. I don't have to relive it, unless I choose to, and then from a more distant viewpoint. Time is a great healer.

Yoga philosophy helped me, realising my place within the story, the role I was born to play. And if I am meant to play it then I may as well try to play it as best I can, knowing that I may inevitably falter at times, but to understand that it is all part of the story anyway. I accept my role; I accept my story. I accept what happened and as time has gone by, I can now see the positives.

Would my daughter and I have been so very close had this story not unfolded as it did for us both? I am not sure we would, although I admit, I could not know this for sure. We are unusually close – we have to be, since I still have to help her to dress or apply her splints. I still get to see her naked at a very vulnerable time in her life, as a teenager. And although I am sure she may not always wish that level of intimate closeness between herself and her mother, I cannot deny that it has brought us closer. If she expresses her annoyance, I remind her that at various times of our lives, we are all vulnerable and need the help of another. That is the way of life – not one of us is invincible. I am sure there will be a time when I will need someone to help me wash or pull up my knickers. And I hope I greet that situation with grace. That I can ask for help, to be vulnerable, and be thankful and respectful that I might receive help, and to receive that help with loving gratitude. Not to feel ashamed or weak or needy. We all need help and we all receive help. That is the truth. To deny that is to deny our basic humanity. To give help is a blessing. To respond with respect and loving kindness to another's vulnerability is an honour. We all give and receive, that is the way of life. I have come to understand, to accept that.

So I came, over time, to accept where I was, to accept where I am. And during that process, I came to experience gratitude and joy and beauty. There was beauty in my life. There was joy. From that place, I could begin to forge a life for myself, decide how I wanted to live my life. I could begin to dream a little…

To accept where I am and move on. Not forgetting the past, but simply to see it as my story, as just stuff that happened. Because that is the truth of it. Stuff happens and stuff happens to everyone. We all grieve, we all suffer, we all experience pain. I do not own the exclusive rights.

To accept my story, to see it as just a story. To understand it means everything and nothing at the same time. That is the place I now more regularly reside in. In yogic terms, I am less affected by the play of the gunas (simplistically described as the forces of inertia/ignorance, movement/energy and peace/clarity). I see them at play, I see them at work, but I don't have to engage or be bothered by them. I can simply observe them, to see them for what they are, and see beauty in their play because they are natural forces – I need not be a part of their play, but I can choose to, if I want to.

So now, if something seemingly appears negative, I know that at some point down the line (or sometimes even immediately), there is another way, another perspective. If I am presented with a particular situation or event, I know there is something I can practice, or that I am to learn from that experience. So, there ceases to be 'good' or 'bad', there just is. And I will learn from what is either way, so I may as well be a willing participant. To go with the tide rather than fight it. To be a participant in carving my own path, rather than being dragged kicking and screaming. That is the path I now try to choose. As if I am slowly and carefully whittling myself into something beautiful, rather than being hacked at, chopped down. I choose to create my-Self.

I aspire to do that with grace, to be a participant in my own growth and evolution.

New Poppy

It was explained to me over Poppy's MRI scan that part of her brain was not working – considered dead. It was easy to see the area of her brain that had died. It was surprising to me that even within hours of having a stroke, in comparison with the healthy textured brain matter, the affected area was already showing in the image as a uniform grey. At this point, Poppy had only recently come from surgery and was still sedated and on a ventilator. I had no idea what sort of 'Poppy' would wake up. Would she still be the sweet girl I had known for the last 23 months? What was to change?

I think my greatest fear was that the sweet girl I knew so well would not come back to me. That her darling disposition would be eradicated somehow. To be quite honest, I wasn't entirely sure how a stroke could affect a person. Now, 13 years later, I have a much clearer idea.

It was a milestone when Poppy was removed from the ventilator. As I have already described, it was already evident that she had difficulty using one side of her body. Her foot was already twisting away. Within a week of becoming more conscious, she was supplied an off-the-shelf Ankle Foot Orthosis (AFO). But what of her character, what of her sweetness? It was hard to tell because she was still quite unwell.

When we were finally discharged seven and a half weeks later, with an ileostomy reversed (thankfully), I remember her first physiotherapy task was to practice rolling over. She was understandably weak. By the New Year, just a few weeks later, she was already walking – a massive achievement that I think demonstrates Poppy's will and determination. These were traits she had always displayed and they served her well in this situation.

We did spend lots of time rehabilitating, but also cuddling. I am sure we are championship cuddlers. I felt she needed that unconditional envelope. It was my intuitive counter to all the trauma.

We were encouraged to get Poppy back to a normal routine so we returned to the toddlers group and some sessions at her local pre-school. Everyone was very supportive.

It was evident that her sweet nature had survived intact. Her character had made it through. But our family dynamic had changed drastically. I wasn't just Mum anymore. I was also an Occupational Therapist and Physiotherapist. The demand on me had grown and grew seemingly exponentially over the years. There was so much to fit into a day, so much to be responsible for. As I have already detailed, I was exhausted. So many times, I had to alter my perception of the situation or redress the reality of our position. Alongside the obvious grieving, the deep sorrow and sadness, was also a frustration and anger. I felt as if my life had been hijacked. I was now so many roles, seamlessly amalgamated, and I was not entirely sure I really wanted any of it, or what of it did I want? My role as parent carer was as comprehensive manager of Poppy's care. That extended to outside of the home. Every medical appointment included updating professionals on the latest news and progress. I was the only person who possessed a 360-degree view. I found it was a precarious role – to be the single most important person in the management of my daughter's care, but simultaneously the least valuable, who could be trumped at any time by my 'unofficial' status. Professionals could play their professional card, I could not. I was a jack of all trades but master of none, to many.

All these unwritten, unspoken and unexpected lessons took their toll in many ways. At times, I have never felt so powerless, so dehumanised, so much an object of curiosity. All I wanted was to secure the right provision for my daughter. It has been quite a trick to do that from one of the most powerless positions, where cold criticism or judgement could come at any time, from anyone, who could out-rank you instantly as an 'expert'. I have learned tact, diplomacy and mastery of strategy. I have felt that I am the only person keeping an eye on the 'long game'. What of the future?

So, there was always a lot going on: obvious and subtle, both had their place. It was a very overwhelming time. I felt overwhelmed most of the time.

What became evidently confusing was how I felt about Poppy. I never felt disappointment. I never felt ashamed. I never felt embarrassed. I never will. That made things much easier, one less internal battle. But I did have to separate out how I felt about Poppy and how I felt about my situation. I love Poppy, but I certainly did not always like my situation, of which Poppy was at the heart. I had to do things I did not want to do. I was naturally shy, I always have been, but I could not be reticent in meetings. I had to speak up and speak out – that was necessary to secure Poppy the right provision or service. I had to learn to defend her situation and advocate for her, but I could not in all honesty say it was my innate nature. I had to learn, grow and develop those skills, for her benefit. It seemed a very strange motivation in many ways. I had to develop for Poppy, not myself. Of course, the reality was that it was for me, because changing for Poppy did benefit me, but it did feel, in the beginning especially, a bit like I was being dragged along. It felt a bit unnatural. Uncomfortable.

Endless, seemingly meaningless form-filling was now another aspect of my life – justifying and making the case for, apparently, everything. It becomes a skill. Apart from the tedium and repetition, some forms can be enormously depressing since you have to detail and outline every single negative thing in your child's life (and consequently your situation). You fill in a form describing everything in detail that your child cannot do, is unable to do or finds difficult to do. I did experience a low mood for some weeks after completing some gruelling forms. That, I guess, is inevitable.

What had my life become? I seemed to have no life. I felt as if my personal freedom was slowly being eroded. I know I described it at times as feeling as if I was being forced into a very small hole – slowly and surely, my space was shrinking. My freedom was slowly departing and it was tough watching it slip away, because I felt I had no choice but to observe. I came to be sick of my life. I felt so thoroughly sick of it.

So to feel that way, I had to be very clear about what exactly I was sick of. I could not be sick of my sweet girl. I could not, could I? That is a path that leads to shame and self-hatred. I very carefully inspected all my feelings. What was I really sick of? Of course it was not Poppy. She had done nothing wrong. She was changed and I needed to grieve 'old' Poppy, the part of Poppy that had departed, which was really a future way of life. Walking together in the woods, skipping just for fun, waving goodbye as she walked herself to school. That was a potential way of life I had to grieve. I had to say goodbye to the more normal expectations of life, of a more normal flow of life, and get acquainted with a new, more alternative, flexible way of living. Let go of the idea that I might work full-time, that a career might depend on that type of set-up. That was just not possible. My grief was like a tumbleweed that grew as time went on, with so many little griefs added on as I met them with 'oh, I hadn't thought of that'.

It perplexed me for some time, considering what I was grieving when it came to Poppy, since she did not die. She did not actually go anywhere, but she was not the same Poppy. She was changed and those changes had brought anxiety, frustration, anger, confusion and a feeling of powerlessness. I knew I had to be very careful to separate out 'Poppy' from the situation surrounding Poppy. I had to be very clear. Then I could express my feelings without experiencing any type of shame. I was not criticising or judging 'Poppy' and it was okay to admit I was sick of my situation. Yes, it was a situation with Poppy at the centre, but she was not responsible for the whirlwind surrounding it. I could still love and adore my sweet girl, and entertain conflicting thoughts about our situation. Both could exist at the same time. That was and is okay.

It also meant I could be very clear to Poppy that she was not the cause of any of my pain or suffering. Of course, it was and is not her, personally, who might cause me discomfort. It is the situation. I am so grateful that I took the time to be clear and clarify my and Poppy's position. But it took some time and there was a period of confusion and overlap, while I transitioned over to new Poppy. For a time, they both existed at the same time: my perception of old Poppy and the reality of new Poppy. It is interesting to grieve what has not entirely been lost, just a part – the part that existed really only in my head as a perception and as a memory. To grieve what was, whilst living with what is. It took time for new Poppy to become just Poppy. Old Poppy no longer exists now. It is like another lifetime ago. Like old Poppy really has died.

It is such a strange conundrum because, in reality, Poppy never went away. She just morphed into a different being, like a butterfly emerging from a chrysalis. Poppy already has transformed – what an amazing achievement. The space that existed, unseen but very tangibly felt, between old Poppy and new Poppy was taken up with grief, but now those two Poppys are in alignment. Poppy is Poppy. I am sure it is easier for her now to just be. We all have our part to play and if I did not grieve for my sense of Poppy then perhaps I would hold back her own grieving. It had to be done, for her benefit as well as for my own. Poppy is responsible for her own grieving process but I do feel I had to provide the safe space for her to do so. I could not bring my own grief into it. It had to be worked through, and so it was. So it is. It is an ongoing process.

There are times when I know Poppy has felt responsible for how I might feel, if I am upset, or maybe that we don't have much money to do things or whatever our situation has and might entail. But at those times, I can reassure her that it is absolutely not her fault. Our situation is not her fault, it is simply a by-product of events that occurred. Again, there is no blame or incrimination, and it's okay to feel crappy about our situation. That is okay. We are allowed to feel crappy. I used to feel more crappy and now I hardly feel crappy at all. But I know Poppy does feel crappy and as she approaches young adulthood, she is facing those cold, hard assessments of her life. There are lots of question marks that I know she would like answered. Will she be able to drive? Will she have a meaningful relationship? Will she have children? Will she be able to live on her own without support, as she so desperately wants?

We all face difficult uncertainties at that age, but I do feel hers are magnified and that is not unreasonable to believe. She has a lot to grieve and a lot to face. I may be able to hide my insecurities, faults and limitations in any number of ways, but Poppy wears hers largely for all to see. She has to be the most brave and courageous. Her will and determination must not falter, in the face of red-tape, discrimination and apathy. So I applaud her all the way. I am her biggest supporter. I will be her life-long cheerleader, because she is going to need that support. My experience of our lives so far has confirmed that. You cannot change the world; you can only learn to live within it. That's not to say that we have failed to experience some amazing things and amazing people, but there is so much selfishness and ignorance too. You have to be realistic. You have to be reasonable. You have to face harsh truths and you have to appreciate the beauty in the world when you notice it. What a blessing my situation is, because that is exactly what I have come to see. Bitter sweet. And that is okay.

My jyotish astrologer (the astrology that accompanies Yoga and Ayurveda, and shares the same core beliefs) once described it along the lines of being capable of happiness even when your life is not perfect. Perfection does not exist, but perfect imperfection does. To simply be, and be content.

To be comfortable with what is. To know deep down, not just to intellectually understand, that everything is okay, that I am exactly where I am meant to be. I have a lot more faith now. I wandered through the wilderness of faithlessness and somehow along the way, I discovered faith. Faith in myself. Faith in my capabilities. Faith in the absolute goodness of the world. Faith in its beauty. It is all there, just for me, if I take the time to see it.

However, I did not always feel that way. There were times when I felt so hopeless that I thought about killing myself, and times when I thought the only logical and very practical conclusion would be to take Poppy with me. What would she do without me? I do not presume that I am irreplaceable, but to have such a pivotal role in her well-being, what would happen to her or those around me if I did kill myself and leave her behind? Perhaps then, taking her with me was the only viable option? I recently joined a research group investigating parent carer thoughts of suicide and homicide. I felt I could contribute to this worthy investigation by being completely forthright about my

51

thoughts and feelings at certain periods of my life. Those darker times were preceded by events or triggers that contributed to feelings of hopelessness. It might have been a gruelling hospital meeting, or a reminder of what my life apparently could have been, or having to watch my lovely girl in pain, suffering.

Whatever the root, my mind meandered towards ending my life. I could not take it anymore. Of course, whilst communicating with the research leader about my experiences and feelings, it was clear that what I was really talking about were times when I needed more support. Times when I was not capable, for whatever reason, of finding my own way out of how I felt. I was in a mental cul-de-sac and I needed a guide. It was less about how the thoughts and feelings manifested: 'I want to kill myself.' It was rather what lay behind that expression. Feeling hopeless and worthless. Feeling like I could do nothing to change the situation. What I was expressing was a desire for change and for that change to be supported. I really just needed some flipping help. But not the help that someone else assesses and makes recommendations for (how modern medicine has chosen to function), but help that I determined and that meant something to me. Help that I was an active author of, not a passive reader of. Because the latter just leads to more powerlessness doesn't it? I think it would have for me anyway.

In some ways, that in itself can be a rabbit warren of confusion. I needed support, my feelings of worthlessness were a cry for help, but who is really there to listen? In our hour of need, we only really have ourselves – that's the lonely truth. Back to the lonely truth. Only I could truly help myself. That's not to say that I did not ask for help, was not assessed for help and did not eventually (with patience) receive some help, but only we can truly throw ourselves our own life-lines. To change that dynamic, I grieved and I rebuilt myself. Like a caterpillar into a chrysalis, I too, like Poppy, had to do my time bundled up in my cocoon of sadness until I could take it no longer, and I was ready to bust out as the sleek new butterfly that I am, my wings quivering with purpose. Poppy's organic transformation took seconds, just a blink of an eye as a blood vessel burst in her brain. My transformation, in contrast, took quite a number of years. I needed to steep. I had to sit in the shit of my own making until I realised that I couldn't stand it anymore. And by shit, I mean the way I thought about the situation, all the self-pity and limited ways of being, the pain and the suffering. I was creating that mental shit. So, guess what, let's create new thoughts, let's see the situation from a different angle, let's see and be differently. Flip that coin over to see the other side and shape something beautiful out of something shit. That is what transformation is. And once you realise you have that capacity, that the coin of possibility you hold in your hand has two sides, it is then that you can choose which side you want to play with. That is transforming. It has transformed my perspective. That is all it really is: perspective.

I truly feel now that I live what I am. I am not here to live in my spare time.

Fatigue

I cannot deny that I sleep a lot, even now with Poppy away during the week term-time. I still have to. I continue to find the situation I am in draining at times, and I need to recharge. I currently need between 10 and 11 hours sleep, although I often only achieve seven or eight. I remember when Poppy was first discharged, I felt I could not get enough sleep. I was putting so much of my attention and energy into her care, and everything that surrounded it, that I was exhausted. When Poppy went to her father's I would try to 'catch up' on sleep, which of course cannot really be achieved. I could only experience transitory respite.

That is why I now try to achieve a consistent level of rest. I have already described how I get up super-early and retire correspondingly early, slightly out of sync with the rest of the world. What I found worked for me was rising early, getting my 'me time' before Poppy arose. It was my preparation period for the day ahead. Practicing more yoga. The magical early morning as the sun rises is when I perform my yoga practice and daily ritual. It is a powerfully energetic time of day and my daily supporting ritual starts each day on the right footing, a thankful footing. I anchor myself in positivity and gratitude for what I have rather than what I have not. It has helped so much in reorienting my perspective. The world is simply a more loving place to be, possessing infinite potential.

It is because I have come to understand my process that I appreciate that if I am too stretched, I can help no one. So I pay attention to my personal self-care, in order that I can extend myself to care for others. I do nourish my body, mind and soul with daily pranayama and yoga, walks in the woods, freshly cooked organic food and early nights. I look after myself in order that I may look after others. Looking after myself has to come first, not in a selfish way, but in a very practical way. I have learned to nourish strength and resilience, in order to share my nurturing spirit with others. There is a limit of course, and the reality is that my capacity to care may extend little beyond Poppy. I have faith that I do not have to save the world – loving and caring for just one beautiful being, my daughter, can be enough. It is enough. Of course it is enough. I hope that those around me, whom I love very much, who may feel abandoned or neglected at times, may understand the limits of being mortal, of my mortality. I only have so much energy to share with others, and I have chosen to direct the majority towards my daughter because her needs are great. That is the truth. In all honesty, for me, I could not choose otherwise.

Self-care and stamina are so important when caring for a loved one, because if that is all you can manage then you enter into a life that offers little respite. You become part of the hidden workforce that has no annual pay-rise, no holiday or sick pay, and your job continues 24/7/365. You have few rights, no boss, scant help, meagre perks or expenses, and a distinct absence of opportunity (the latter I found by far the most debilitating). You are on minimum wage and that is that. I am not meaning to appear ungrateful; I fully understand in many ways how I have been so incredibly supported and that my life could have been very different if I had been born into a different time or place on this planet. I am not naive, but I can use my intellect to see both sides of the argument. I acknowledge the amazing opportunity I have been given to be able to cease employed work and be supported by my community to care for my child. It is truly a gift, but that exists at the same time as the constraint and sheer limitation of that gift. The two can and do co-exist.

What I feel I have done, not intentionally at first, but eventually, was to see the merit in that constraint and limitation, to actually see where I could grow personally within it. It was not a growth that could be seen, but I hope can be experienced by others. I can give back for all that I have been given, but I am not using the normal currency or exchange that many people value. I have learned the currency of pure love. I personally feel that is the highest goal and to me, it's the most valuable currency of all. Money can bring enormous opportunity, but it inevitably has its limits because it is a creature of the physical world. The currency of love has no limit. I may be paid in the currency of man, but I transform it into the currency of the divine. I value and cherish that. As I have written, not everyone shares my values. I can be considered a sponge to society: I take and give nothing. It depends on your perspective and what you value as to what you see as my purpose.

What of Poppy? She might be viewed as the ultimate drain, drawing 'public' money to pay for care, or education, or to supplement any future lack of income. She could be criticised by others for that, by those who do not share our values. Or she could be emulated for her sheer courage and bravery in standing opposite to that, in all her tender vulnerability. Knowing and intensely feeling her individual limitation, but keeping faith in her inherent value, the value she was born with and holds, nourished I hope, until she departs this life. The value in being a human being on this planet, willing to learn and grow. Just because we have created a powerful value system based upon printed paper (or now plastic), that does not mean that she may only be measured against it. There are so many other value systems we might be measured against. I measure her against the value system of the divine, the value system of love. Against that, she more than measures up and is more than worthy of her space in this world.

It depends on your perspective.

I believe we can choose how we greet the world: with friendliness, with forgiveness, with love, with courage to be ourselves, with compassion for others. I believe we can give each other a break because we all suffer, we all grieve, we each feel our individual experience intensely.

Future

The same astrologer who told me I had spent lifetimes exploring, learning and growing, also told me that I was pulling all those strands together in this lifetime.

So, what do I think I have learned? That I am on a spiritual path. Poppy's illness was an abrupt wake-up call to everything that was truly important rather than what I thought was important. There can often be a difference between what we think and what we know or feel.

I have learned patience, tolerance, determination, pace and above all, faith. Faith in myself. Faith in a benevolent universe that supports me in all that I do. Even if my experience has seemed harsh, unrelenting or unforgiving. That is only what it seems from a certain perspective and I have learned that there are many perspectives, an infinite number of perspectives. May I learn to see the lesson and move on to the next. May I learn to look at something and see what it really is, and let go of my personal perspective, of any perspective I may bring to any given situation, which may colour that situation. Like wearing coloured spectacles. May I remove them to see clearly. To see what is.

I hope I do. I trust that I will.

This book, for what it is, is one step in that direction. My intention in writing this was to write something true. True to me. I know full well that this is my perspective of events, circumstances and relationships. We all have our own unique perspective. I wanted to write without fear of reprimand or of criticism. To write without censor, my own censor or the censorship of anyone else. Not to feel ashamed of my thoughts and feelings, to accept them as they were and as they are. We experience so much, I did not want to deny any of it, because it is all me. We are all so much.

Whether seemingly positive or negative, what I feel, all of it, is legitimate. Every single feeling has its place, there is nothing to deny or cover up. What I have been doing is finding my place within those feelings. When I see that my mind is so fragile and contrary, I need not be so concerned when it tries to run away with me (in the form of thoughts). I simply need to try to hold onto a stable place and stay anchored. I can anchor myself in what is, rather than where my mind may wish to take me. Our minds are so powerful, they hold such capacity for change and transformation. I am learning to take charge of my own mind. If I can achieve that then I can begin to steer my path. To carve the path that I have been born to take. My path, my unique path, the one only I can take. To whittle myself into something beautiful. Carved by sorrow and pain into something uniquely, beautifully exquisite.

But beyond that, I have been learning to grieve, and it is well worth my time to grieve. To process my pain and suffering. Writing this, I have experienced so much recurrent grief, but I realise not quite so acutely. It is okay to look at it. I feel it is healthy to do so. I feel it would be detrimental to my overall health and well-being to shy away from my feelings of loss. Where would they go if I did not process them? It is okay to feel vulnerable, to feel hurt. It is okay. I remember we all hurt, we all cry. It is part of our human condition. It is part of be-ing. We all need, we are all helped. That is so beautiful to acknowledge. I am isolated and connected all the time. I reach out and I am reached out to. Bitter sweet. I see both sides and everything in between, and accept it all. I can sit between the opposites and accept them both as being true at the same time. To acknowledge the beauty within the pain and the pain within the beauty. To hold them in balance and sit with them in the same moment. Perhaps that moment is grief.

To know there is no right and no wrong, simply experience. So to me now, everything is okay. I cannot make a wrong decision because every path is the path of growth and discovery. I accept that the path I took was exactly right for me because it's the path I take. I am exactly where I am meant to be.

What of the future for Poppy and myself?

For Poppy, hopefully to enjoy a renewed love of learning. To achieve enough to be accepted at college and if she chooses, to go on to study at university. Poppy aspires to be an author – what an amazing story she could write. A story as extraordinary as she is. I trust that whatever features in her future is going to be extraordinary, it seems the only logical conclusion. I will look forward to watching her story unfold, to watch her unfolding. Opening to her beauty and pain. I am excited to witness it.

For myself, I wish to use my experience as a parent carer to help others in a similar situation. To challenge the more accepted categorisation of Cerebral Palsy (it's not always confined to just the physical aspect) to foster greater understanding of the condition, ultimately leading to better support.

To guide others to reach their potential, whatever that may be for them. I gain much satisfaction from accompanying others towards their goal, even if I am not actually there to see them achieve it. Just to witness someone finding their way is hugely satisfying to me.

To teach yoga, which has become such a huge support to me in my life. To be able to pass on some of what I have learned about yoga and its philosophy. It has such potential to transform. I know it has transformed my mind and I know I have much to transform ahead of me. I am so grateful to have the support to transform through yoga.

I wish to live in the woods, in a fully accessible dwelling that meets all of Poppy's needs. With space for a yoga studio and an Ayurveda treatment room, and an equipment room for Poppy and a study for her to write in. With space for all the things she needs to live as independently as possible. For her to live in ease. To live closer to nature in peace, calm and abundance. That, I know, will feed my soul. How I get us there I do not know, but I trust that I am already taking decisive steps in that direction. Our future is already being built by us and for us.

To write more. I have much to share.

To continue to grow. To continue my own transformation, wherever that takes me. I am excited to find out where my story takes me. Far I hope.

To do all that whilst I support my girl, first and foremost. Always to support my girl, because she is the light. That is my core purpose.

She is the love of my life and to her, I devote all of myself. Everything with so much love. It is overflowing and unending.

That place I discovered during her illness, so vast and wide and full of despair. I now realise as I write, it's also so full of love.

A love so vast and wide, so limitless.

Postscript

I'd like to thank all those persons I felt confident enough to share this with in its early stages. I'd also like to especially thank Becky Skuse for casting her editorial eye over this final version.

I had started to edit this collection of muses again, but today, the 1st of January 2022, I decided to let it be. Let this remain a snapshot in time. A reflection of where I was when I wrote this and importantly what I thought, roughly four years ago.

I realised if I edited once more, it would be with my current mind, along with all that I have learned since I wrote this. And what a time I have had, especially the last couple of years! I almost cannot put into words what the response to COVID19 has meant to Poppy and myself. We have once again been challenged in profound ways and I have found myself stretched in almost all directions. I have been gifted with another opportunity to grow! So, today, on reflection, I decided to let be what was and is, and offer this up to you to read, to digest, to discard, to pass on, to recycle, whatever you feel is right for you. Many blessings to you.

Lisa